FLOWERS

# SUNFLOWERS

John F. Prevost
ABDO & Daughters

Published by Abdo & Daughters, 4940 Viking Drive, Suite 622, Edina, Minnesota 55435.

Printed in the United States.

Cover Photo credits: Peter Arnold, Inc.
Interior Photo credits: Peter Arnold, Inc.

Edited by Bob Italia

**Library of Congress Cataloging-in-Publication Data**

Prevost, John F.
      Sunflowers / John F. Prevost.
        p.  cm. -- (Flowers)
      Includes index.
      Summary: Provides brief information about the various parts of the sunflower plant, as well as varieties, pests, diseases, and economic uses.
      ISBN 1-56239-611-0
      1. Sunflowers--Juvenile literature. [ 1. Sunflowers. ] I. Title. II. Series: Prevost, John F.  Flowers
      QK495.C74P74  1996
      583' .55--dc20
                                   96-1179
                                       CIP
                                       AC

# Contents

# Sunflowers

Sunflowers belong to the 15,000-member aster and daisy family. Sunflowers were first grown in North America. They may be **annuals** or **perennials**.

Annual sunflowers are easily started from seeds. They will grow, bloom, and make seeds for only one season. Perennial **varieties** are grown from seeds, **rhizomes,** or **tubers**. Perennials grow year after year.

Native Americans grew sunflowers for food, dyes, and decoration. Today, sunflower varieties are grown worldwide for food, oil, and their beautiful flowers.

*Opposite page:*
*The sunflower is a*
*giant among flowers.*

# Roots, Soil, and Water

Sunflowers pull water from the ground with their roots. The roots also keep the plants from falling over. All sunflowers have large root systems. The roots find water and **nutrients** the plants need to grow.

Sunflowers will grow in different soil types, but do best in moist, **fertile** soil. The deep root system allows the plant to survive in dry soils or areas where people walk. Too much or too little food or water will reduce the flower's quality.

Sunflower roots and seed **hulls** give off a **poison** that hurts other plants and keeps their roots away. In a garden, sunflowers are often planted alone or with plants that can compete with them.

---

*The sunflower's long roots allow it to find water even in dry soil.*

# Stems, Leaves, and Sunlight

The stems and leaves are the parts of the sunflower that grow above ground. Sunlight is important to green plants. Their leaves use it to make food. This process is called **photosynthesis**.

The stems support the leaves and allow them to receive sunlight and water. Stems send water from the roots to the leaves, where food and **oxygen** are made. The food then returns to the roots.

Some sunflower **varieties** such as mammoth, jumbo, and giant gray stripes have long stems. They can grow more than 10 feet (3 m) tall.

# Photosynthesis

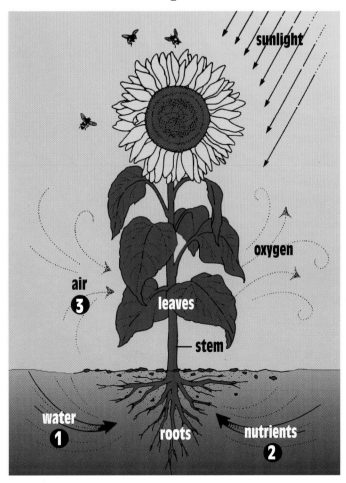

Ground water (1) and nutrients (2) travel through the roots and stems and into the leaves where air (3) is drawn in. Then the plant uses sunlight to change these three elements into food and oxygen.

# Flowers

Sunflowers are popular because of their large **blossoms**. Each blossom is actually a **flower head** made of many flowers held together.  The blossoms can be 2 to 12 inches (5 to 30 cm) across.

Smaller flowers are found on the multi-stem sunflowers. The largest flowers grow on the single-stem **varieties.**

Each small flower has two main parts: the **stamen** and the **pistil**. The stamen makes the **pollen** that insects and wind carry to other sunflowers. The pollen **fertilizes** the pistil's **ovules**, which become seeds.

The sunflowers' blossoms are well-known for following the sun. The flowers and leaves face east in the morning (sunrise) and west in the evening (sunset). That is why they are called sunflowers!

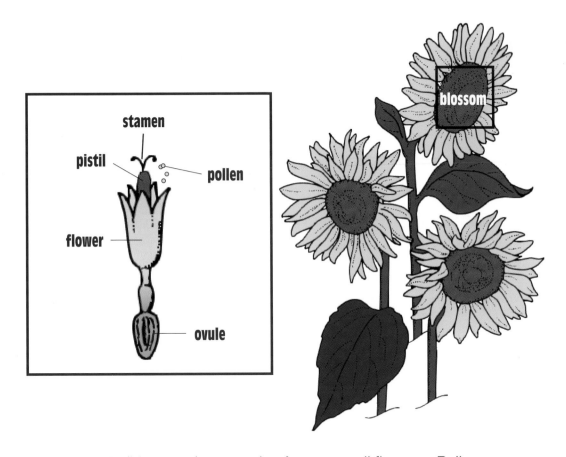

Flower heads (blossoms) are made of many small flowers. Pollen from the stamen fertilizes the pistil's ovules. The ovules then grow into seeds.

# Seeds

Most **annual** sunflowers are grown for
their seeds.  These seeds are used for their oil or for
use as human or animal food.

The seeds grow in the large **flower head.** After
the **petals** have fallen off, the seeds continue to
grow and eventually dry.  The seeds protect and
make food for the tiny plant **embryos** inside them.

**flower head**

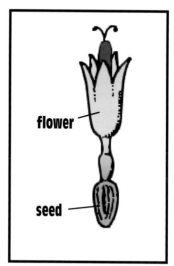

**flower**

**seed**

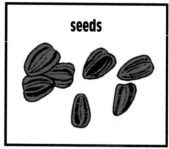

**seeds**

After the ovule turns into a seed, the seed continues to grow until it dries. Inside each seed is a tiny plant embryo that will one day grow into a sunflower plant.

# Insects and Other Friends

Sunflowers grow large flower heads to attract insects from great distances. Bees, butterflies, wasps and other insects help **pollinate** sunflowers. While feeding on the flowers' **nectar**, **pollen** sticks to their legs. The insects spread the pollen when flying from flower to flower.

Sunflowers also attract other animals. Many **predatory** insects such as ladybugs, lacewings, and wasps live on these plants and eat **pests**. Spiders also live on the leaves and stems. They eat the plants' enemies and do not harm them.

*Bees help pollinate sunflowers by carrying pollen from flower to flower.*

# Pests and Diseases

Sunflowers attract several types of insect **pests.** **Aphids** and white flies can be a problem in the garden. Weevils, caterpillars, and beetles also damage the seeds. Often, **predatory** insects and spiders keep these pests under control.

Many birds and **mammals** will try to eat the sunflower's seeds. The large **flower heads** act as feeding perches for these animals. To keep them away, netting, bags, and frightening devices like scarecrows are used.

**Diseases** will attack the flower head and **stalk**. Keeping sunflowers healthy is the best way to fight disease.

*A field of sunflowers.*

# Varieties

There are more than 150 sunflower types in North America. The giant **annual** sunflower is the most popular.  It is grown for its seeds, which are used as food. The seeds are a rich source of **minerals.**

**Varieties** have been raised for different needs and uses.  Some have seeds that contain oil used for cooking.  Other varieties are grown for their flowers. Others are grown for unusual leaf or flower colors.

Swamp sunflowers, thin-leaved sunflowers, willow-leaved sunflowers, and Mexican sunflowers are grown in wildflower gardens and as single plantings. Many are **perennials** and will grow back year after year.

*Sunflowers have a variety of colorful flower heads.*

# Sunflowers and the Plant Kingdom

The plant kingdom is divided into several groups, including flowering plants, fungi, plants with bare seeds, and ferns.

 Flowering plants grow flowers to make seeds. These seeds often grow inside protective ovaries or fruit.

 Fungi are plants without leaves, flowers, or green coloring, and cannot make their own food. They include mushrooms, molds, and yeast.

 Plants with bare seeds (such as evergreens and conifers) do not grow flowers. Their seeds grow unprotected, often on the scale of a cone.

 Ferns are plants with roots, stems, and leaves. They do not grow flowers or seeds.

There are two groups of flowering plants: monocots (MAH-no-cots) and dicots (DIE-cots). Monocots have seedlings with one leaf. Dicots have seedlings with two leaves.

The aster and daisy family is one type of dicot. All sunflower varieties are part of the aster and daisy family.

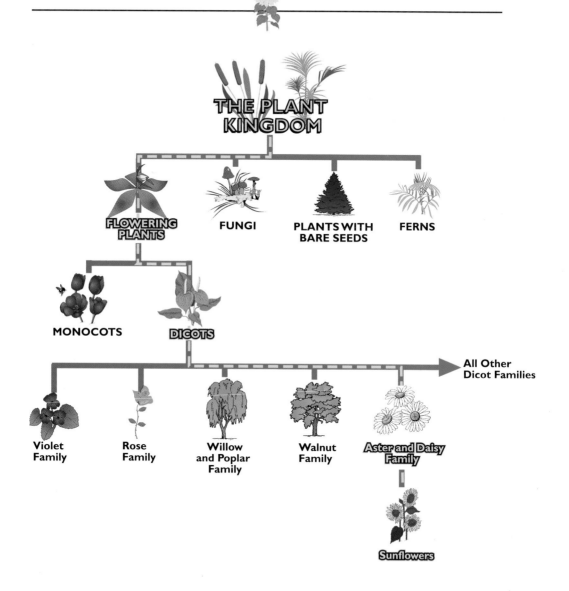

# THE PLANT KINGDOM

FLOWERING PLANTS

FUNGI

PLANTS WITH BARE SEEDS

FERNS

MONOCOTS

DICOTS

All Other Dicot Families

Violet Family

Rose Family

Willow and Poplar Family

Walnut Family

Aster and Daisy Family

Sunflowers

# Glossary

**annual** (ANN-yew-ull) - A plant that grows from a seed, matures, and dies in a single season.

**aphid** (AY-fid) - A small insect that sucks the sap from plant leaves and stems.

**blossom** (BLAH-sum) - The flower of a plant.

**disease** (diz-EEZ) - A sickness.

**embryo** (EM-bree-oh) - An early stage of plant growth, before sprouting from a seed.

**fertilize** (FUR-tuh-lies) - To develop the ovule into a seed.

**flower head** - Many small flowers held together.

**hull** - The outer covering of a seed.

**mammal** - Warmblooded animals with a backbone that feed their offspring milk.

**mineral** - Any substance that is not a plant, animal, or another living thing.

**nectar** - A sweet fluid found in some flowers.

**nutrients** (NEW-tree-ents) - Substances that help a plant grow and keep it in good health.

**ovule** (AH-vule)- A seed before it is fertilized by pollen.

**oxygen** (OX-ih-jen) - A gas without color, taste, or odor found in air and water.

**perennial** (purr-EN-ee-ull) - A plant that lives for three or more years.

**pest** - A harmful or destructive insect.

**petal** (PET-ull) - One of several leaves that protect the center of a flower.

**photosynthesis** (foe-toe-SIN-tuh-sis) - The use of sunlight to make food.

**pistil** - The female (seed-making) flower part.

**poison**- A substance that is dangerous to life or health.

**pollen**- A yellow powder that fertilizes flowers.

**pollinate** (PAHL-ih-nate) - The use of pollen to fertilize a flower.

**predator** (PRED-uh-tore) - An animal that eats other animals.

**rhizome** (RYE-zome) - An underground stem with roots.

**stalk** - The main stem of a plant.

**stamen** (STAY-men) - The male flower part (the flower part that makes pollen).

**tuber** (TOO-burr) - The thick part of a root used for food storage.

**varieties** (vuh-RYE-uh-tees) - Different types of plants that are closely related.

# Index